Revealed:
A Kingdom Journey
By
Cynthia Alvarez

PUBLISHED by PARABLES
Earthly Stories with a Heavenly Meaning

Revealed: A Kingdom Journey
Cynthia Alvarez

Published By Parables
February, 2019

All Rights Reserved. No part of this book may be reproduced or utilized in any form or by any means, electronic or mechanical, including photocopying, recording, or by any information storage and retrieval system, without permission in writing from the author.

    ISBN 978-1-945698-96-5
    Printed in the United States of America

Readers should be aware that Internet Web sites offered as citations and/or sources for further information may have been changed or disappeared between the time this was written and the time it is read.

Revealed:
A Kingdom Journey
By
Cynthia Alvarez

Earthly Stories with a Heavenly Meaning

Revealed: A Kingdom Journey

CONTENTS

Chapter One
The Groundwork Begins Here
Page 5

Chapter Two
Born to Be Great
Page 15

Chapter Three
He Ordered My Steps
Page 25

Chapter Four
The Wrong Direction
Page 35

Chapter Five
From Victim to Victor
Page 47

Chapter Six
Reminded of His Love
Page 55

Chapter Seven
Thanks Be to God Who Gave Us Victory
Page 63

FOREWORD

The journey that life sets before us can be challenging as well as uncertain in many ways. As a result of various struggles and hardships, we as believers are oftentimes left in a baffled state of mind without the ability to make sense of life. The reason it might seem this way to us is because without insight, understanding, and truth, we are only experiencing life through a nearsighted spectrum. Unfortunately, when life is experienced through such a limited perception, it always reveals an insufficient cultivation of our faith, hope, and love, which are the inner forces in our lives that bridge the gap to maturation. And when maturation is realized, destiny materializes. But, if these forces are not being cultivated in our daily lives, we will remain in a continual cycle of frustration and defeat.

The goal of this book is to give insight, understanding, and truth that will help in the cultivation of faith, hope, and love within you, while also allowing you to measure the breadth of every experience you face in life. As these inner forces begin to develop in you, every experience and obstacle of life will begin to fall into place like pieces of a puzzle that reveal a much broader picture when placed in proper alignment. The essential purpose and usefulness of the many challenges in life will become clear to your understanding, as you are finally able to make sense of everything that life has presented to you. Being able to make sense of life is a sign of maturation, and maturation is always the prerequisite for the manifestation of destiny. Are you ready to meet your destiny? Are you ready to rise in maturation? If so, this book will not disappoint you. Get ready to move beyond the uncertainty of life's challenges and into the glory of your destiny!

Blessings,
Cynthia Alvarez

Chapter One
The Groundwork Begins Here

There is nothing more elusive to the mind of any person than trying to understand a comprehensive truth of life's journey with a limited knowledge base. It is no secret that man is limited in his mental capacity and unable to grasp the infinite mysteries of life without God bridging the gap to make it possible. Yet, even with a divine way having been made for him to come into a more complete and excellent mental stature in God through the death, burial, and resurrection of Jesus Christ, man must still be compelled to pursue the greater realities of life. For this reason, God has extended a greater dimension of himself among believers with the indwelling of His Holy Spirit to not only become resident in us, but to also aid us in developing a greater mental capacity to understand the totality of all that He has freely given to us by His Spirit. Except God brings the increase to our mental capacity by the work of His Spirit in us, we would remain mentally deprived and ignorant of our very own heritage in Christ.

"Now we have received, not the spirit of the world, but the spirit which is of God; that we might know the things that are freely given to us of God." (I Corinthians 2:12)

The development of a greater mental capacity is of the utmost importance for us because it is the very groundwork that makes it possible for us to accommodate the work of His Spirit and retain the spiritual deposits that are imparted to us. But without this essential development, we could never put the pieces of life's journey together to make sense of it all. So, there becomes a need for us to be hard-pressed in every facet of our being, which usually comes in the form of trials and troublesome circumstances that we are led into by His Spirit to yield the necessary results of expanding our mental faculties as God deems enough. In other words, our lives must be turned upside down and inside out to make room for continual spiritual deposits or divine impartations that bring unprecedented increase and enrichment to our mental state.

"We are troubled on every side, yet not distressed; we are perplexed, but not in despair. Persecuted, but not forsaken; cast down, but not destroyed; Always bearing about in the body the dying of the Lord Jesus, that the life also of Jesus might be made manifest in our body."   *(II Corinthians 4:8-10)*

This is the method that God has chosen to bring us into a place of unlimited knowledge, unhindered truth, and the unequivocal stature of His greatness that will also allow us to discover our own greatness in Him. In fact, it is the only way that we become fully capable and qualified to stand in the fullness and greatness of His Kingdom as heirs and joint heirs with Christ. We must have the mental competency level of kings possessing a Kingdom which has been appointed to us by the sovereign King of Kings in all regality, prudence, and power.

"And I appoint unto you a kingdom, as my Father hath appointed unto me; That ye may eat and drink at my table in my kingdom and sit on thrones judging the twelve tribes of Israel." (Luke 22:29-30)

It is impossible for us to remain mentally challenged in our progressive understanding of life's greater truths because these truths bring us into a reality of the Kingdom of God. As we come into the reality of the Kingdom, we come into the reality of the greatness of God within ourselves even during the many tribulations and perils encountered. Through embracing truth and enduring what we might consider hell on earth in various hardships and trials, we begin to see something miraculous taking place within us as we become witnesses to the ever-increasing development of our own mental bandwidth in ways we knew not of. The truth of God becomes nourishment to our hearts and minds which causes our will to become submissive to His will for our lives. It helps us understand and recognize the frailty of our own mental condition apart from the power and reality of God in our lives. Except God intervenes in our lives, we are without understanding and hope. We are as ships tossed about by the waves of the sea that become beaten and battered by the elements of this world, with no safe harbor to find shelter or rest. It is God alone who establishes us in Christ, enriches us through His Spirit, and validates us in His Kingdom. Don't let anyone beguiled you into thinking otherwise.

"Now he which stablishes us with you in Christ, and hath anointed us, is God; who hath also sealed us, and given the earnest of the Spirit in our hearts."
(II Corinthians 1:21-22).

There is a deep yearning within the heart of every person for the ability to make sense of all that we encounter in life, whether good or bad. No one enjoys living on the blind side of life without the capacity to discover who they are and why they are here. People love to discover more about themselves even if they do not readily admit to it. They love to discover how they look and how they measure up to others. Just take a glance in anyone's home in your neighborhood and you will discover that every home has several mirrors. Why? The truth is that people want to see themselves as they really are; discover things outwardly about themselves that will in some way help give them a glimpse of who they really are deep within, while simultaneously attempting to make sense of it all. But the only problem with trying to discover who we are by looking in a mirror without the truth that is found only in God, is that we are stifled and limited in our viewpoint. In fact, the only image we can possibly see is just a blurred reflection of ourselves that at most is filled with vanity of the mind; and can only satisfy a limited and underdeveloped mental capacity. Except we partake of His knowledge and wisdom through the truth of His word and through revelation by His Spirit, we are walking without the very power needed to transform our lives into God's absolute standard of greatness which is attained in Christ alone.

"But when that which is perfect is come, then that which is in part shall be done away. When I was a child, I spoke as a child, I understood as a child, I thought as a child; but when I became a man, I put away childish things. For now, we see through a glass, darkly; but then face to face; now I know in part; but then shall I know even as I am known." (I Corinthians 13:10-12)

After realizing that the mirror can only show them an outwardly vain and blurred image of themselves and nothing more, they begin to search for deeper truths of who they are through the lives of others. In doing so, they begin to define their own conceptuality of who is great, while determining idealistic guidelines that they think will lead an individual into the acquisition of greatness. However; such reasoning can only result in us measuring ourselves by the standards of man and judging our successes and failures by the lives of others, which makes it impossible for anyone to reach the altitude of God's immeasurable greatness and will continue to keep us at a suppressed mental capacity level.

"For we dare not make ourselves of the number or compare ourselves with some that command themselves: but they, measuring themselves by themselves, and comparing themselves among themselves, are not wise." (II Corinthians 10:12)

It is without debate that man is little to nothing except God transforms his life and molds him into something more. There is no questioning God's ability to take nothing and make it into something greater. He specializes in wonders. After all, He is the same God who called the universe into existence from absolute nothingness. He is the same God who formed man from the very dust of the earth. He is the same God who calls those things that be not as though they were. He is the same God yesterday, today, and forevermore. He is a God of increase and desires to bring increase to every dimension of our lives.

"What is man, that thou art mindful of him? And the son of man, that thou visit him? For thou hast made him a little lower than the angels, and hast crowned him with glory and honor. Thou made him to have dominion over the works of thy hands; thou hast put all things under his feet." (Psalm 8:4-6)

How does He bring increase to our lives? Through a simple principle: God will never deposit into us what He cannot harvest out of us. Every spiritual deposit that He makes in our lives is an investment that is meant for the sole purpose of producing a Kingdom return. Whether it is a spiritual gift imparted to you or a spiritual fruit produced in you, it will bring increase to your life. It will transform your life, so that you can walk in power and authority that you have never experienced before. This transformation is not just for you, but it is necessary for God's power, wisdom, love, knowledge, etc. to flow through you and out to others to bring change to our society. God has an objective that He shall accomplish in your life and through your life which has the capability to impact people, cities, nations, and kingdoms. He is placing deposits of greatness in you, so that He can harvest greatness out of you. Understand that whenever God calls us to a Kingdom work or objective, it is always a call to greatness because a Kingdom mandate or assignment is not just about winning individual souls into the Kingdom, but about bringing nations, kingdoms, and governments under the sovereign rule of God. The mandate is a two-fold work by which we will bring the nations to God and bring God to nations. It is a large- scale work that requires a large scale or fully developed mentality. It is not just a great work, but it is also a great mystery that cannot be taken lightly, nor can it be committed to the unequipped. The Kingdom of God can only be entrusted to Jesus and those who have the qualifying credentials to join Him as joint heirs of the Kingdom.

"And the seventh angel sounded; and there were great voices in heaven, saying, the kingdoms of this world are become the kingdoms of our Lord, and of his Christ; and he shall reign forever and ever." (Revelation 11:13)

Understanding the importance of the condition of our mental capacity as it relates to moving us into the Kingdom of God and the acquisition of our eternal inheritance is the ultimate- goal of this book. We must not only realize that His Kingdom is upon us now, but we must be proactively engaged in its full manifestation. It is not enough for the Kingdom to be formed within us, it also must be manifested outwardly, visibly, and tangibly in the earth. Jesus came to earth over 2000 years ago to pay the penalty for the sins of the world through His death, but because of His resurrection, He was able to deposit the Kingdom of God within us through the work of His Spirit. Yet, when He returns, He is coming to receive a fully manifested Kingdom that has been made ready for the King of Kings in every aspect. Knowing this shall come to pass as God has foreordained, we are to be in a continual state of preparation and looking for the imminent return of our Great King. Even so, my earnest desire is that this book will enlighten, empower, and instill within your hearts, the truth that is in Christ concerning the King and His Kingdom, as well as our vital role as heirs. For this cause, I am intently compelled to persuade you to be diligent always in Christ, while eagerly preparing yourself as a bride adorned for her groom's sudden arrival. Make ready your hearts and minds to receive your eternal King and His eternal Kingdom. Be ye ready because the groom is eager to meet His bride. After all, He has waited over 2000 years to receive her to Himself. So, make no mistake about it, the bride is admonished to prepare herself because Jesus is expecting to receive a fully developed and fully equipped bride capable of ruling by His side in the Kingdom. With such expectations, it is no surprise that He has provided us with all that we need through His Spirit to bring us into a stature that is worthy of Christ and worthy to be in Christ. We must take advantage of everything that has been placed in us and all that is set before us by His Spirit, as it is able to make us abound richly in all things pertaining to God and the Kingdom, so that we are found deficient in no area of our lives. Let nothing hinder you from being ready or cause you to forfeit your inheritance in Christ.

"Even as the testimony of Christ was confirmed in you: So that ye come behind in no gift; waiting for the coming of our Lord Jesus Christ: Who shall also confirm you unto the end, that ye may be blameless in the day of our Lord Jesus Christ." (I Corinthians 1:6-8)

"According as his divine power hath given unto us all things that pertain unto life and godliness, through the knowledge of him that hath called us to glory and virtue; Whereby are given unto us exceeding great and precious promises: that by these ye might be partakers of the divine nature, having escaped the corruption that is in the world through lust." (2 Peter 1:3-4)

Cynthia Alvarez

Chapter Two
Born to Be Great

In the previous chapter, we discussed the groundwork that must take place within our lives to position us for Kingdom increase, since not everyone who is born into this world is born to be great or even called to greater. For many people, greatness is simply not in their gene pool. Yet, given certain opportunities and perhaps knowing the right people could place them at an advantage over others to some degree. Thus, giving them a sense of self-pride, some level of self-worth, and an air of self-confidence that can only be measured by a small temporal moment in time. But on the flip side of that coin, everyone who has been born again by His Spirit is born for greatness and born into greatness because we have been born into a Kingdom that is greater than any kingdom in the universe. It is the eternal Kingdom of our eternal God. Not only are we born into the Kingdom as new creatures in Christ, but we are born into an heirship as sons of God or sons of destiny who are privileged to walk before God as kings and priests in the Kingdom. Think about that for a minute. There is no greater heritage to receive than that which we are afforded by being born again into His eternal Kingdom.

"But, as many as received him, to them gave he power to become the sons of God even to them that believe on his name: Which were born, not of blood, nor of the will of man, but of God." (John 1:12-13)

"For whom he did foreknow, he also did predestinate to be conformed to the image of his Son, that he might be the firstborn among many brethren." (Romans 8:29)

Although we are born into greatness and the Kingdom set before us, unless we ultimately know who we are, whose we are, and what we are called to inherit, we will never possess the Kingdom. We will never be able to walk as kings and priests because we cannot possess what we cannot grasp. Nor can we grasp what we are not made aware of. How can we become great when we know nothing about greatness? We can only become great when God takes the initiative to extend greatness to us through revelation of His will for our lives. The moment He makes His will for our lives known to us or the moment we are made aware of our destiny, the process to greatness begins for us. This very process can be seen demonstrated through the life of Joseph as he received revelation from God of his impending and exceeding great destiny that was delivered by means of a prophetic dream. Through the dream, God made known to Joseph that he would stand in a place of power, dominion, and great favor one day. In fact, it was even revealed that his entire family would bow before him in that day. Because God had taken the initiative and extended greatness to him through revelation, Joseph knew without a shadow of a doubt that he was not only born to rule, but also to reign in life.

"And Joseph dreamed a dream, and he told it his brethren; and they hated him yet the more. And he said unto them, Hear, I pray you, this dream which I have dreamed: For, behold, we were binding sheaves in the field, and lo, my sheaf arose, and stood upright; and behold, your sheaves stood round about, and made obeisance to my sheaf. And his brethren said to him, Shalt thou indeed have dominion over us? And they hated him yet the more for his dreams, and for his words." (Genesis 37:5-8)

"And he dreamed yet another dream, and told it his brethren, and said, Behold, I have dreamed a dream more; and, behold, the sun and the moon and the eleven stars made obeisance to me. And he told it to his father, and to his brethren: and his father rebuked him, and said unto him, what is this dream that thou hast dreamed? Shall I and thy mother and they brethren indeed come to bow down ourselves to thee to the earth?" (Genesis 37:9-10)

His confidence was not in what he told himself about his own life; his confidence was in what God had revealed to him about his life through a prophetic dream. The very nature of the dream itself was powerful, progressive, and interwoven in sovereignty. It had the ability to change not only the course of Joseph's life, but it was powerful enough to shift his perspective about himself and those around him. From that moment forward, no one could discredit what God had imparted into the heart and mind of Joseph. Greatness had been imparted to Joseph through the Holy Spirit. As a matter of fact, this moment was the very inception of his divinely orchestrated journey to a destiny which was so great that we still make mention of his life until this day, while acknowledging the power of God operating through him to save multitudes near and far. Joseph was not called to save only his family, but it was clear that God had a greater mandate for him that encompassed multitudes from across the land. He was called to fulfill a Kingdom assignment and was therefore able to preserve not only his family, but other nations also who needed what he had to offer them.

"And his brethren also went and fell down before his face; and they said, Behold, we be thy servants. And Joseph said unto them, Fear not: for am I in the place of God? But as for me, ye thought evil against me; but God meant it unto good, to bring to pass, as it is this day, to save much people alive." (Genesis 50:18-19)

Understanding that the nations needed what Joseph had to offer them allows us to see that the principle God uses to bring increase in our lives is infallible. (God will never deposit into us what He cannot harvest out of us.) It is obvious that the magnitude of Joseph's destiny required him to have the mental stature of a king which meant God would have to allow a continual flow of spiritual deposits or impartations in his life. There was no other way that Joseph could have attained to such an elevated position except God empowered him by transforming his life to make him suitable to rule a kingdom and governor nations. It would have been an impossible thing to accomplish had he not been hard pressed on every hand. He had to endure what could have easily broken his walk with God, if he had not been given insight into who he was and what the will of God was for his life. Joseph was able to endure all things because of the joy that had been set before him or should I say because of the revelation God had given him about the greatness of his destiny. We can see this same operation of the Spirit in the life of Jesus who endured all things for the joy that had been set before Him too, concerning His unparalleled destiny.

"Looking unto Jesus the author and finisher of our faith; who for the joy that was set before him endured the cross, despising the shame, and is set down at the right hand of the throne of God." (Hebrews 12:2)

Although everyone who is born again has been born into greatness and born for greatness, we must all mature into greatness. There is no magic trick that will make us great without the work of God in our lives. Each of us must take our own journey to greatness. It is a progressive journey that only God can accompany us on because He is the one who makes the necessary spiritual deposits in our lives along the way, so that we might grow in His knowledge and grace.

"According as his divine power hath given unto us all things that pertain unto life and godliness, through the knowledge of him that hath called us to glory and virtue." (2 Peter 1:3)

From the onset of this journey, we must be willing participants from start to finish even as Joseph was. There is no cutting corners or shortcuts in reaching our destiny, especially when it is saturated in such greatness. Faith and endurance are key components that we must all possess and demonstrate as we move onward. Without these components operating in our lives, we would fall miserably short of achieving our physical place of greatness and our mental state of greatness in the Kingdom. In other words, we would be unable to fulfill the Kingdom assignment that God has intended for us. We would not be suitable to impact nations, kingdoms, and governments to bring them under the rule of God's Kingdom which is the sole purpose of any Kingdom assignment. In our best effort, we would only be able to impact a few local individuals because our reach and influence is always predicated on what we have allowed God to do in us and through us. The more we allow God to do in us by transforming us into the image of His son Jesus Christ, the greater our reach will be across the globe. For Jesus declared that our works in the earth would be emphatically greater than what we even know. He was making it plain to our minds that we are called to the Kingdom to be great and to do great things.

"Verily, verily, I say unto you, He that believeth on me, the works that I do shall he do also; and greater works than these shall he do; because I go unto my Father. And whatsoever ye shall ask in my name, that will I do, that the Father may be glorified in the Son. If ye shall ask any thing in my name, I will do it." (John 14:12-13)

We must never forget that Joseph had to have the mental stature of a king in order to govern nations. He had to have wisdom, insight, and knowledge that could only come from an intimate relationship with God. His mind and heart had to be so interwoven with God, that everywhere he went and everything he did, God accompanied him along the way. It did not matter where he was at any given moment on his journey; the only thing that mattered was that God was right there with him. The presence of God makes the difference in our lives and Joseph knew it. So, it did not matter that he was sold to the Midianites, purchased by Potiphar to be a servant in his home, thrown in prison for false accusations, or standing before Pharaoh himself, God was with him and caused everything he did to prosper. He was able to cause Joseph to prosper in everything because Joseph allowed God to transform his life in every circumstance that he faced. Joseph trusted that God was great enough to perform that which had been revealed to him in the prophetic dream. The presence of God with

Joseph made it possible for him to endure all things. It also gave Joseph the opportunity to see God's abundant favor manifested in his life.

"And the Lord was with Joseph, and he was prosperous man; and he was in the house of his master the Egyptian. And his master saw that the Lord was with him, and that the Lord made all that he did to prosper in his hand. And Joseph found grace in his sight, and he served him: and he made him overseer over his house, and all that he had he put into his hand." (Genesis 39:2-4)

"And Pharaoh said unto Joseph, Forasmuch as God hath shown thee all this, there is none so discreet and wise as thou art; Thou shalt be over my house, and according unto thy word shall all my people be ruled: only in the throne will I be greater than thou. And Pharaoh said unto Joseph, See, I have set thee over all the land of Egypt." (Genesis 41:39-41)

This should be the very desire of each of us as we journey onward to the greatness of our destiny with God accompanying us along the way. Nothing that we face should cause us to lose confidence in who we are and what we have been called to inherit, after God has revealed it to us. Yet, we must continue to be mindful that the moment we become aware of His will for our lives, the process to greatness begins. This process will be elaborated on in the following chapters to open your understanding of the totality of all that you have faced previously, currently, and will face futuristically on this journey. So, you might know that greatness comes with a great price, but it also yields an even greater reward.

Cynthia Alvarez

Chapter Three
He Ordered My Steps

In Chapter Two, we elaborated on how God moves us into greatness, as there is no other way for us to reach a Kingdom destiny without being divinely empowered or enhanced to accommodate a greater spiritual bandwidth. So, we will not get to destiny on a whim, nor will we stumble upon it of our own accord. It is like a prized possession that must be pursued, as well as a hidden treasure that must be discovered. There must be a wide display of effort and a revealing of mature faith on our part to reach the plateau of our destiny. Yet, we cannot get there unless God ushers us through the very door of destiny.

"The steps of a good man are ordered by the LORD; and he delights in his way. Though he falls, he shall not be utterly cast down: for the LORD upholds him with his hand." (Psalms 37:23-24)

It is clearly a joint effort that gets us there because we must work together with God to accomplish something on such a glorious plateau as reaching our destiny. He has measured and meted out our steps and created a sure path for each of us to embark upon that will undoubtedly place us at the doorstep of destiny. Not only has He created the path that we are to travel, but He is the overseer of our journey. Through the life of Joseph, we can clearly see that God was the one who governed his path. Every step that he took was saturated in the purpose of God. How do we know that it was saturated in the purpose of God? Because no matter where Joseph went on his journey, God elevated him amid every circumstance he would face. Even so, God will not have us to be ignorant concerning the unusual manner of promotion in Joseph's life. Make no mistake about it, the nature of Joseph's promotions was not only progressive, but each promotion was a sovereign act of God alone.

"For promotion cometh neither from the east, nor from the west, nor from the south. But God is the judge; he puts down one and sets up another." (Psalms 77:6-7)

God had tempered together everything and everyone on Joseph's journey in such a way that every encounter, every person, and every obstacle proved beneficial for him despite how it might have looked at first glance. It was all working towards a greater weight of glory for him. In other words, God had big plans for Joseph. God was setting him up and setting him apart for a work of Kingdom proportion. Everything Joseph endured was with the intent of him fulfilling God's Kingdom agenda, and so it is with each of us who have been chosen in this hour. Many things that we endure at times can seem meaningless and unjust amid the struggles and hardships of life, as we tend to become near sighted and unable to see beyond our immediate circumstances. But if we could only look past our right now circumstances, we would see the bigger picture and understand that we are on a collision course with an exceptional destiny that demands a major overhaul of our lives. Just as Joseph's life had to be overhauled and uniquely conditioned for the high-ranking role of his Kingdom assignment, so must our lives be subject to the same requirements.

"For our light affliction, which is but for a moment, worketh for us a far more exceeding and eternal weight of glory." (II Corinthians 4:17)

Joseph was being strengthened and conditioned by God for the journey that was set before him just as an athlete in a race is equipped and conditioned to run at his full potential to seize the victory that awaits him at the finish line. The athlete is not being prepared to lose, but to win. For this reason, God was conditioning Joseph for the utmost victory which required **spiritual enhancement**, **mental soundness**, and **physical fitness**. He was being equipped with every essential attribute needed to ensure his rise to prominence and stripped of every unnecessary weight that would prevent his progression towards greatness.

"Wherefore seeing we also are compassed about with so great a cloud of witnesses, let us lay aside every weight, and the sin which doth so easily beset us, and let us run with patience the race that is set before us." (Hebrews 12:1)

Joseph's **spiritual enhancement** could be recognized as he was put in various situations that caused him to exercise his spiritual gifts and solve the problems of others. The use of his spiritual gifts magnified God amid a nation that knew nothing of Joseph's God. Through his life, he was able to bring his God to the nation of Egypt, as well as bringing many surrounding nations to his God by way of Egypt.

"And Pharaoh said unto his servants, can we find such a one as this is, a man in whom the Spirit of God is? And Pharaoh said unto Joseph, Forasmuch as God hath shown thee all this, there is none so discreet and wise as thou are: Thou shalt be over my house, and according unto thy word shall all my people be ruled; only in the throne will I be greater than thou." (Genesis 41:38-40)

His **mental soundness** was evident in his disciplined lifestyle which made it easy for others to trust him in matters of administration. Joseph's character was exceptional and garnered him favor in many circumstances. Even after being rejected by his brothers, falsely accused by Potiphar's wife, and forgotten by the butler in prison, his Godly character remained consistent. Although the Egyptians had not known the God whom Joseph served, they were able to see God through the very character of Joseph.

"And he left all that he had in Joseph's hand; and he knew not ought he had, save the bread which he did eat. And Joseph was a goodly person, and well favored." (Genesis 39:6)

Joseph's **physical fitness** was exemplified in the fact that he had survived the hardships of his entire journey from the pit to the palace. He lived to the good old age of 110 years and was able to see his children of the third generation.

"And Joseph dwelt in Egypt, he, and his father's house: and Joseph lived a hundred and ten years. And Joseph saw Ephraim's children of the third generation: the children also of Machir the son of Manasseh, were brought up upon Joseph's knees." (Genesis 50:22-23)

Every step that Joseph took on this journey was filled with divine purpose, as each step yielded experience that would ultimately work for his good and the preservation of the world. There was nothing he had endured that was not interwoven into the very fabric of his destiny. In fact, every disappointment and every setback were prerequisites to reaching the plateau of greatness. Although this was a journey to greatness, the path that had been set before Joseph was not to be equated to a bed of roses, but rather likened unto a wilderness path filled with thorns and thistles because it was a path that no one had traveled before. It was a path that had been tailor-made for him alone. Likewise, it holds true for each of us, God has prepared a path that we must travel alone if we desire to reach our destiny. It is a path we have not traveled before, so we can never think that we will be able to reach the end of that path or even understand the purpose within it, apart from God. Clearly, this was not a path that Joseph could travel with anyone other than God. There were no exceptions allowed, and neither would God change the method of fulfilling His plans for Joseph.

For the first time in his life, Joseph would be separated from his family and the only life he had ever known. He would have to leave behind everyone and everything that had previously held a place of importance in his life. In fact, the only things that could accompany him along the way were the intangible things that were instilled in him by his father, Jacob, and the things that had been deposited in him by God. Joseph received a rich intangible heritage that could never be taken from him because it was 100% spiritual in essence; therefore, he was able to access it at any given moment and in any place. God had given him full access to the wisdom, knowledge, revelation, and insight that was necessary for each situation he encountered. Joseph had been richly endowed by God through the Spirit.

"The LORD is the portion of mine inheritance and of my cup: thou maintain my lot. The lines are fallen unto me in pleasant places; yea, I have a goodly heritage. I will bless the LORD, who hath given me counsel: my reins also instruct me in the night seasons. I have set the LORD always before me: because he is at my right hand, I shall not be moved. Therefore, my heart is glad, and my glory rejoices: my flesh also shall rest in hope." (Psalms 16:5-9)

What had God placed in Joseph to sustain him on his journey? God had deposited the substance of greatness in Joseph and his steps were being ordered in compliance with God's will of elevating him to the plateau of greatness. Yet, what many have failed to realize is that although God had originally deposited the substance of greatness within the heart of Joseph, God also had to pull or draw greatness out of Joseph and make it become a reality. The pulling and drawing of greatness out of our lives is usually the most unpleasant part of the journey for us. Of course, we enjoy the presence of God with us, His favor resting upon us, and blessings overtaking us, yet when it seems as if the tables have turned and we are faced with insurmountable pressure, unwavering challenges, and an onslaught of troubles in life, the journey to greatness seems to figuratively become more of a journey through hell. Nevertheless, how the journey makes us feel along the way can never be compared to who we become at the completion of the journey.

"For I reckon that the sufferings of this present time are not worthy to be compared with the glory which shall be revealed in us. For the earnest expectation of the creature waits for the manifestation of the sons of God." (Romans 8:18-19)

We must understand that the path Joseph traveled was not an easy path, but it was infused with thorns and thistles because it was a path of pruning, molding, and renewing. There was no other path that he could have taken to secure his appointment with destiny. Not only is destiny a place we are striving to reach, but it is also a precise moment in time that must be seized. It is a place and time where the manifested will of God in Heaven becomes a reality on earth and within our lives. Our destiny will always manifest the will of God on earth because it will always advance His Kingdom in such a way that a new dimension of glory is released, and this glory will never allow us to go back to who we were before our journey began. Therefore, He releases new dimensions of glory into our lives to give place to the manifestation of the Kingdom of God that is being formed within us. If the Kingdom of God is not within us, it will never become a physical reality for us because only what is in us will be harvested out of us. For this reason, God is always concerned with making spiritual deposits or impartations in our lives. He is putting the Kingdom in us, so that we can manifest it through our lives. We must never underestimate or despise what God places in us because what is placed in us is a mystery that is progressively being revealed to us and through us. Although the Kingdom is deposited within us in a mystery or unseen form, it is the absolute evidence and authentic substance of the Kingdom abiding in us to empower us in carrying out the sovereign will of God.

As we look at the path of Joseph's journey, there is one constant thread throughout the whole of his experiences. That thread was God and He is the one who ordered every step that Joseph took. Although, the things he endured seemed unfair and it almost appeared that injustice was Joseph's lot in life, nothing was further from the truth. The journey to Joseph's destiny was a journey of transformation and exaltation because it revealed who he always was in the eyesight of God and where he was always meant to be in the plan of God. During this journey, his life was altered, shifted, and renewed in many ways. God was using circumstances that had been divinely orchestrated to transform the mind, heart, and status of Joseph. Yet, the culmination of his journey was his rise to prominence and power in a land that had not known the God whom Joseph served until his journey led him to that place.

"And all countries came into Egypt to Joseph for to buy corn; because that the famine was so sore in all lands." (Genesis 41:57)

There is no questioning the nature of Joseph's destiny whatsoever. His destiny was to fulfill a Kingdom assignment by bringing God not only to Egypt, but to the nations of that day. His reach was indeed far and wide in fulfilling the work of God. God had ushered him into a place or a standing of royalty for the work of the Kingdom. It was a high call, and it was a costly call for Joseph. Although he had lost many things on the journey, he gained so much more because of who had ordered his steps and accompanied him on the journey.

"Trust in the LORD with all thine heart; and lean not unto thine own understanding. In all thy ways acknowledge him, and he shall direct thy paths." (Proverbs 3:5-6)

Chapter Four
The Wrong Direction

In Chapter Three, we were able to recognize the importance of allowing God to order our every step on this Kingdom journey, since following the divine path that He has strategically established for our lives is the only hope we have of ever reaching the door of destiny. If we would take a moment to think about our lives, most would agree that nothing is more frustrating than investing precious time and effort into an endeavor, only to find out that it did not make the cut and must be discarded entirely. Not only must it be discarded, but we must now start over from the very beginning, with the same goal of being successful at it the second time around. This really should sound familiar to all born again believers because this is exactly what we have had to do. Before we were saved and born again, we lived the best way we knew how, according to the knowledge, traditions, and experiences we had partaken of. We did the best we could apart from a genuine relationship with God, which is the reason we lived to only please ourselves. But when we were born again and made the choice to live for God, our old life had to be scrapped or discarded because it fell short of His plan for us. We were on a path of unrighteousness that was leading us in the opposite direction of the destiny and inheritance that awaits us. It was a path that appeared to lead us in the right direction and was completely congruent with fulfilling our own will. The decisions that we made, connections we had, and goals we were trying to reach all seemed ideal for ourselves, except none of it was in alignment with the will of God, nor could it lead us to the destiny that He has prepared for us.

"There is a way which seems right unto a man, but the end thereof are the ways of death. Even in laughter the heart is sorrowful; and the end of that mirth is heaviness." (Proverbs 14:12-13)

We were clueless and without understanding of all that His will entailed as it regarded us. Yet, God has always been intent on fulfilling His will in our lives. In fact, from the moment we were born again, He has been taking the necessary measures to align us with His perfect will, or it might be best to word it in a more descriptive manner by saying, "God has been making epic moves in order to correct and preserve the destinies of all those who are a vital part of His Kingdom agenda." He has been busy stripping our mindsets of our own reservoir of self- indulged ideas and goals that exclude any reference toward the King or the Kingdom. Without question, we were headed in the wrong direction and in need of a divine extension of grace to realign every aspect of our lives with His perfect will. Yet, this sounds much easier than it really is, especially when the process of realignment for your life blindsides you, as it tends to come in the manner of a striking and sudden impact. Most of us were just minding our own business and going about our daily routines, when something came out of nowhere and turned our lives upside down and inside out. We did not see it coming, nor did we have an explanation for it. But it was clear from the start that our lives would forever be altered by this dramatic introduction of the realignment process, which had now gripped our hearts and minds. This is the same reality or experience that Joseph had encountered while minding his own business and going about his daily routine. He was simply following the instructions of his father as usual, when out of nowhere, he became blindsided by the realignment process; his life was turned upside down, inside out, and forever changed.

"And it came to pass, when Joseph was come unto his brethren, that they stript Joseph out of his coat, his coat of many colors that was on him; And they took him and cast him into a pit: and the pit was empty, there was no water in it. And they sat down to eat bread: and they lifted up their eyes and look and behold, a company of Ishmeelites came from Gilead with their camels bearing spicery and balm and myrrh, going to carry it down to Egypt. And Judah said unto his brethren, What profit is it if we slay our brother and conceal his blood? Come, and let us sell him to the Ishmeelites, and let not our hand be upon him; for he is our brother and our flesh. And his brethren were content. Then there passed by Midianites merchantmen; and they drew and lifted up Joseph out of the pit and sold Joseph to the Ishmeelites for twenty

pieces of silver: and they brought Joseph into Egypt." (Genesis 37:23-28)

Joseph did not wake up on this peculiar day with expectations of being stripped of his coat of many colors that he had received from his beloved father or being sold into slavery at the hands of his own brothers. If he had known what would befall him that day, there is no doubt that he would have made the appropriate preparation to avoid the unforeseen actions of his brothers. I am 100% certain that if he had known what would have transpired in his life on that day, Joseph would have taken the necessary precautions to protect himself from the cruelty of his brothers by exposing their evil intentions to his father.

"But know this, that if the good-man of the house had known in what watch the thief would come he would have watched and would not have suffered his house to be broken up." (Matthew 24:43)

Yet, Joseph felt no need to approach his brothers in a precautionary manner. After all, they were his family and he had obviously gone to visit them at work on many occasions, according to his father's instructions. Never had he felt the need to be cautious when going into the presence of his brothers before. So why was this day any different than any other day when visiting his brothers? This day was different because it was an appointed time on the divine schedule of God that would cause the will of God to supersede the will of Joseph and disrupt his way of life. It was this precise moment in time that God decided things could no longer continue as they had been in the life of Joseph. It was the day that God would execute His detailed plan to correct and align the destiny of Joseph with His sovereign will. Although the day did not transpire as Joseph had imagined it would, the day had exemplified the will of God in the divine execution of His purpose. Sometimes at our own comprehensive level, things can seem like a chaotic mess when unforeseen circumstances interrupt the normal flow of our lives. But at God's level of comprehensiveness, things that seem chaotic and disruptive to the flow of our lives are usually the perfect working of His plan for us.

"For my thoughts are not your thoughts, neither are your ways my ways, saith the LORD. For as the heavens are higher than the earth, so are my ways higher than your ways and my thoughts than your thoughts." (Isaiah 55:8-9)

As God's plan took root in Joseph's life, we can see that he had surrendered completely to the will of God. Never do we read that Joseph tried to escape from any experience he endured after the realignment process for his life had begun. The bible never mentions Joseph trying to escape and return home to his family at any point of his journey. He was sold to the Midianites, sold to Potiphar, falsely accused by Potiphar's wife, and thrown into prison, but not once does the bible mention him ever trying to escape. Why not? Although Joseph did not understand the full scope of the things he was enduring, he knew that God was with him, and that God had meted out his steps. As long as he was obedient by adhering to the will of God for his life, Joseph did not see the struggles he faced through a defeatist mentality. Instead, he saw them as milestone accomplishments as he journeyed with God to a destiny that was divinely prepared for him. He did not see himself as a victim of circumstances, but instead saw himself as a victor of promises achieved. Not only was Joseph walking out the plan of God for his life, but his very life would become a testimony for others to follow throughout the ages.

"This he ordained in Joseph for a testimony, when he went out through the land of Egypt: where I heard a language that I understood not." (Psalms 81:5)

He was not only a pioneer of faith, but through his life the power of God was manifested for all to see. For only the power, wisdom, and authority of God could take Joseph from the place of a lowly pit, set him apart from others, and elevate him to a place of sovereignty. Some might question the sovereignty of his authority, yet Pharaoh had placed total administration of the Kingdom of Egypt into the hands of Joseph. Joseph's words became the law of the land because Pharaoh had entrusted him with the affairs of Egypt. Pharaoh did not keep up with the governing details of the nation, it was Joseph who did. In fact, Pharaoh was not involved in any of the governing aspect of the nation of Egypt once Joseph was elevated to the seat of power. Pharaoh held a title of authority, but Joseph possessed and exercised the power of Pharaoh's seat of authority.

> *"Thou shalt be over my house and according unto thy word shall all my people be ruled: only in the throne will I be greater than thou. And Pharaoh said unto Joseph, See, I have set thee over all the land of Egypt. And Pharaoh took off his ring from his hand, and put it upon Joseph's hand, and arrayed him in vestures of fine linen, and put a gold chain about his neck; And he made him to ride in the second chariot which he had; and they cried before him, Bow the knee; and he made him ruler over all the land of Egypt, And Pharaoh said unto Joseph, I am Pharaoh, and without thee shall no man lift up his hand or foot in all the land of Egypt."*
> *(Genesis 41:40-44)*

After seeing the power and wisdom of God operating through Joseph, Pharaoh knew that Joseph was more qualified to govern the nation than he was himself. He understood that Joseph could do for Egypt that which he could not do for Egypt. Pharaoh understood that Joseph was not like any man he had ever encountered before. He knew Joseph was a great man, with or without a title. He not only knew, but he believed that Joseph had the ability to make Egypt the most prominent nation in the world. So, he was not hesitant about entrusting the nation into Joseph's hands. Furthermore, we can see that Pharaoh's level of trust in Joseph did not come from Joseph's outward qualities, but it came because of what he recognized on the inside of Joseph. Pharaoh was able to see and experience the undeniable power of God through his encounter with Joseph. In fact, the encounter had such a powerful and lasting impact on Pharaoh that he was motivated to make one of history's greatest political moves to date. He wanted to ensure that the presence of Joseph's God would continue to remain in Egypt for the duration of his lifetime, so Pharaoh decided that it was more befitting and beneficial to place Joseph in the seat of absolute authority in the kingdom. By doing so, in no uncertain terms, Pharaoh was in all actuality inviting God to govern Egypt because he knew that the Spirit of God was the true source behind Joseph's wisdom, knowledge, and revelation. He was making a strategic move that would propel the nation to the forefront of the world. By placing the governing power of Egypt into the hands of Joseph, Pharaoh was undoubtedly turning the Kingdom over to God, as it was evident that God was with Joseph and would be ruling the nation through him.

"And Pharaoh said unto his servants, can we find such a one as this is, a man in whom the Spirit of God is? And Pharaoh said unto Joseph, Forasmuch as God hath shown thee all this, there is none so discreet and wise as thou art." (Genesis 4:38-39)

The course to destiny and the place of destiny for Joseph were both defined by His intimacy with God. The course to destiny showed his love and commitment to God as the two journeyed together from start to finish, while the place of destiny showed his commitment and diligence to the work of the Kingdom as he saved the lives of multitudes and preserved nations. Joseph was so fixated on his destiny and fulfilling the absolute will of God that even when his father and brothers came to abide in Egypt, Joseph placed them in the best of the land, yet he remained in Egypt, in the marketplace of the world, and among the nations where the seat of his destiny was.

"And Joseph placed his father and his brethren and gave them a possession in the land of Egypt, in the best of the land, in the land of Rameses, as Pharaoh had commanded. And Joseph nourished his father, and his brethren, and all his father's household, with bread, according to their families" (Genesis 47:11)

We understand that Joseph was the favored son of his father, Jacob, and had been given profoundly prophetic dreams by God. But he would not have made it to his seat of destiny unless God stepped in, realigned his life, put him on the right course, and made achieving destiny possible for him.

"And he said, the things which are impossible with men are possible with God." (Luke 18:27)

Once Joseph had arrived at his seat of destiny, he was unwilling to forsake or compromise the work of God for anyone. Yes, Joseph loved his family dearly which is why he made sure they had everything they needed when they arrived in Egypt. However, Joseph never put anything or anyone ahead of the Kingdom work that God had entrusted to him. God knew that the well-being of

Joseph's family was important to him, so He made it possible for Joseph to be in a position that would allow him to not only save multitudes, but to also provide for the needs of his entire family, as the wealth and resources of Egypt had now become fully available to him. He had unlimited access to the riches of that Kingdom. In this we can to see God's faithfulness as he reciprocated immeasurable grace to Joseph, in response to Joseph's notable stewardship to Him. As Joseph was diligently working on God's behalf for the sake of the Kingdom, God was diligently working on Joseph's behalf to secure his family and preserve future generations.

"But as for you, ye thought evil against me; but God meant it unto good, to bring to pass, as it is this day, to save much people alive." (Genesis 50:20)

There is no difficulty in recognizing that the all-encompassing sovereign will of God had been at work in every facet of Joseph's life and He is doing the same manner of work in our lives as well. As we pursue the Kingdom of God and move closer to the seat of our destiny, we can see God positioning us in such a way that our families and future generations have also been included in His Kingdom plan. In fact, our lives become the very avenue that He will use to sustain them and secure their place in His Kingdom. He has graciously made room for not only us, but those who are dear to us, as we pursue that which is dear to Him; His Kingdom.

"But seek ye first the kingdom of God, and his righteousness; and all these things shall be added unto you." (Matthew 6:33)

Cynthia Alvarez

Chapter Five
From Victim to Victor

Previously, we discussed what happens when we find ourselves moving in the opposite direction of our Kingdom destiny and contending with frustration. As we struggle with the power of frustration, it comes as no surprise that we might frequently feel as though we have become victims of unfavorable circumstances. Oftentimes it might appear as if life is a revolving door, which keeps us in a continual cycle of trials and struggles that seemingly increase in intensity with each step we take. It's not that we love being in this place of continuity, we just find ourselves up against familiar and recurring opposition that perhaps is more relentless than our own passion for progress. Do not misunderstand me, I'm not saying that our passion is not fervent whatsoever, but I am saying that the opposition or enemy has added another element to his passion that gives him the upper hand in many instances. This additional element is aggression. And when you interject aggression into any situation involving opponents who are vying for dominion, it can give leverage to the one exerting it.

"And from the days of John the Baptist until now the kingdom of heaven suffers violence, and the violent take it by force." (Matthew 11:12)

It is important to recognize the innate difference between passion and aggression because passion without aggression is just a strong feeling or desire. It's just a particular manner of intense thinking that is the result of certain feelings and it requires no proactive effort on an individual's part. But passion with aggression produces a powerful and assertive force of action. In other words, aggression has progressive power that can change situations for those who are willing to exercise it. Unfortunately, many born again believers don't exercise aggression in challenging situations that arise in their lives, which usually leaves them feeling like defeated victims. In all honesty, they find it difficult to understand why circumstances do seldom yield the desired results that they seek. But the question I want to pose to them is, "Were they just thinking fervently about how they want things to go when confronted by the opposition? Or were they on the move and taking the fight to the opposition instead? Clearly, the manner of which one faces a challenging situation will usually determine the outcome he/she receives. In fact, all born again believers should be walking in victory upon victory because our victory first begins in Christ. We are not victorious because of what we are able to do of our own ability, but we are victorious because of what Christ has already done for us, as He has equipped us with everything necessary to conquer the oppositions in our lives.

"And having spoiled principalities and powers, he made a show of them openly, triumphing over them in it." (Colossians 2:15)

Unless we understand the source and weight of our victory, we will never truly partake of His victory and all that He has accomplished for us. I believe without a shadow of a doubt that Joseph understood the source of his victory was God, which allowed him to face every situation with confidence and assurance. I believe his confidence in God made him eager at times to conquer situations that no one else could overcome. Joseph was just the kind of believer whom God could use at any given moment because he never focused on the size of any problem he encountered. Rather, he focused on the source of his victory in all things. God was his continual focal point.

"And Pharaoh said unto Joseph, I have dreamed a dream, and there is none that can interpret it: and I have heard say of thee, that thou canst understand a dream to interpret it. And Joseph answered Pharaoh, saying, It is not in me: God shall give Pharaoh an answer of peace." (Genesis 41:15-16)

The importance of exercising aggression in dealing with our opposition is that when we exercise it in conjunction with our passion, we are making a bold declaration to not only the enemy but to ourselves. We are confidently proclaiming that we will not become a victim of circumstances, nor will we allow the enemy to dictate the way in which we view ourselves ever again. Too often believers have allowed the enemy to confine them to a victim mentality. It becomes one "woe is me" after another. From that point forward, we see nothing but defeat and negativity which soon turns into extra baggage in our hearts and minds because we have nurtured it with an overextension of attention. Instead of moving ahead, we are too weighted down by the baggage that we have allowed the opposition to drop off in our lives which comes in the form of hurt, insecurities, guilt, fear, anger, abandonment, rejection, low self- esteem, and so on.

"Wherefore seeing we also are compassed about with so great a cloud of witnesses, let us lay aside every weight, and the sin which doth so easily beset us, and let us run with patience the race that is set before us." (Hebrews 12:1)

Let's be clear, when we are carrying around excessive baggage in our lives, it does not matter what door of opportunity God opens for us, we are too consumed with the weight that we are carrying to move onward and through that door. How does the baggage become a weight? It becomes a weight because it becomes a burden to your mind and anything that burdens your mind, burdens your heart. When your heart is burdened and negatively affected, it can easily be seen in your decisions and actions. Doing the things that you need to do which are usually in your best interest, become more difficult to accomplish because now your feelings control the decisions you make. Unfortunately, the feelings that result from harboring excessive baggage will be the feelings that hinder progress, stifle growth and resist the call to destiny.

"For the good that I would I do not: but the evil which I would not, that I do. Now if I do that I would not, it is no more I that do it, but sin that dwelleth in me. I find then a law, that, when I would do good, evil is present with me. For I delight in the law of God after the inward man. But I see another law in my members, warring against the law of my mind, and bringing me into captivity to the law of sin which is in my members." (Romans 7:19-23)

Joseph had endured much negativity and hardship from the hands of others. Although he could be categorized as a victim, he never accepted that title in his heart. No matter what he faced or what measure of ill treatment he had encountered, Joseph didn't hold on to the hurt that he had experienced on his journey. His relationship with God had only been strengthened amid it all and his desire for his life was what God desired for him. There was no mistake about it, Joseph knew that God desired the absolute best for him and he wanted the same thing for his life. So, instead of embracing or focusing on the negative aspects of many of his less than ideal circumstances, he always made a conscious decision to look for the good that could be discovered from each situation. But we must understand that the key for Joseph to discover the good in these unpleasant situations was his ability to navigate his focus. He had to discipline himself in order to position his focus towards finding the good that was present in all circumstances. Let's be honest, many of us have endured things that didn't seem to produce one ounce of good or the slightest inkling of hope in them. Yet, there is always some good in any situation and if we are willing to discipline our mind to become accustomed to detecting or discerning good, we would never be victims of any circumstance. How can we discipline our focus? We discipline our focus by training our minds to look beyond what the natural senses detect. The goal is to train our minds to focus on what we want to discover, not what we naturally see on the surface of any situation. We should be constantly training our minds to go deeper and higher than only the limited perception of our natural senses through focusing on good news, good thoughts, and good experiences. It should be all good.

"Finally, brethren, whatsoever things are true, whatsoever things are honest, whatsoever things are just, whatsoever things are pure, whatsoever things are lovely, whatsoever things are of good report; if there be any virtue, and if there be any praise, think on these things. Those things, which ye have both learned, and received, and heard, and seen in me, do: and the God of peace shall be with you." (Philippians 4:8-9)

Joseph became a master at directing his focal point because his thoughts always reverted to God in every situation, which resulted in God showing His grace or goodness to Joseph amid it all. Joseph's disciplined focus provoked God to demonstrate His goodness openly on his behalf. No matter what circumstances arose in Joseph's life, immeasurable grace always abounded towards him. He could in no way be considered a victim of circumstances because every outcome proved contrary to what we define as a victim. (**victim**: a person harmed, injured, or killed as a result of a crime, accident, or other event or action.) In fact, Joseph proved to be anything but a victim, as we see him triumphant in every situation that could have defeated him.

Potiphar's House:

"And his master saw that the Lord was with him, and that the Lord made all that he did to prosper in his hand. And Joseph found grace in his sight, and he served him: and he made him overseer over his house, and all that he had he put into his hand." (Genesis 39:3-4)

Prison:

"And the keeper of the prison committed to Joseph's hand all the prisoners that were in the prison; and whatsoever they did there, he was the doer of it. The keeper of the prison looked not anything that was under his hand; because the Lord was with him (Joseph), and that which he did, the Lord made it to prosper." (Genesis 39:22-23)

Pharaoh's House:

"Thou shalt be over my house, and according unto thy word shall all my people be ruled: only in the throne will I be

greater than thou. And Pharaoh said unto Joseph, See, I have set thee over all the land of Egypt." *(Genesis 41:40-42)*

The above scriptures allow us to clearly see that Joseph was not a victim in any way. He was simply allowing God to use his life as a demonstration of His love, power, and wisdom to work all things together for our good. Joseph was a willing participant in the plan of God, which would categorize him as a victor in every circumstance that he encountered. (**victor**: a person who defeats an enemy or opponent in a battle, game, or other competition). Only someone who has disciplined his focus in such a way that he is able to identify the good in any situation will be allowed to partake of the richness of God's grace, amid the most unfavorable circumstances. Victims don't get this opportunity because they cannot see beyond the agony of their circumstances, nor have they disciplined their focus to search for the good and beneficial aspect of the thing that they are enduring. While victims are always searching for sympathy, real victors are always reaching for destiny. Remember, it is a matter of choice. You either choose to be a victim or you choose to become a victor. You either choose to train and discipline your focus or you become a victim of your circumstances.

Chapter Six
Reminded of His Love

As we journey onward to destiny, we learn that our circumstances do not define us, nor do they have control over us unless we relinquish our power to them. When we stand firm in who God is and who we are in Him, our stance is always that of a victor. Being saturated in His love and power gives us the assurance that we are always more than conquerors through Christ. Furthermore, nothing will ever compare to the measure of God's love towards us. In fact, the defining factor that moves us to a relentless pursuit of reaching destiny is the excessive love that God presents to us on the path we must travel. It's not the journey that motivates us to keep moving forward, nor is it the tangible riches that are attached to it, but it is His love that compels us to continue forging ahead. If you do not believe me, just take a glance at the world today. Read the headline stories in the news and you will find many rich, famous, and well- to-do people who are committing suicide for various reasons. To the average person, these people might seem like the epitome of a successful life's journey. They appear to have all the essentials that would substantiate having an exceptional quality of life. In fact, they naturally seem to be winning at life. But how can they win at life by making the ultimate decision of taking their own lives? It's simple. Our lives are not successful or blessed because we have an overabundance of tangible riches. Our lives are successful and blessed because of whose we are and what we have been rightfully given through Him. The people that we read about in the news headlines are not committing suicide because of what they have. Rather, they are committing suicide because of what they do not have and what they cannot buy with their material riches.

"For what shall it profit a man, if he shall gain the whole world, and lose his own soul? Or what shall a man give in exchange for his soul?" (Mark 8:36-37)

We have been given unlimited wealth in the spirit that allows us to partake of all the intangible blessings that God has made available to us. No amount of riches or fame will ever be able to trump the love we become privy to in God. There is no measure of earthly wealth that can purchase the peace, love, joy, and comfort that we receive by His Spirit. These are spiritual fruit that are not derived from material essence, so they cannot be found on a shelf at the local market. No, they are immaterial in essence; therefore, they must be experienced in and through a life that is knitted together with God. Our lives must be knitted together with God in such an affixed way that nothing is able to penetrate the intimate bond we have with Him. It is a relationship and bond that supersedes any relationship or bond that we will ever experience in this present age.

"For I am persuaded, that neither death, nor life, nor angels, nor principalities, nor powers, nor things present, nor things to come, nor height, nor depth, nor any other creature, shall be able to separate us from the love of God, which is in Christ Jesus our Lord." (Romans 8: 38-39)

God desires to give Himself to us in every way possible because He wants us to be replicas of Him in all aspects of our being. He is so intent on giving Himself to us in full measure, that He has knitted us together in Christ and placed all the secrets of Himself in Christ, so that we might be partakers of the fullness of who He is.

"For in him dwelleth all the fullness of the Godhead bodily. And ye are complete in him, which is the head of all principality and power." (Colossians 2: 9-10)

"And he is the head of the body, the church: who is the beginning, the firstborn from the dead; that in all things he might have the preeminence. For it pleased the Father that in him should all fullness dwell." (Colossians 2:18-19)

Accomplishing a work of such caliber is made possible because of who He is and all that He is. Furthermore, the only way that we can experience such intangible spiritual essence is that God must allow us to partake of it by way of His Spirit. It is through His Spirit that we have the means to tap into His heart, mind, and power. So, those of you who feel that there is no need to be indwelled by His Holy Spirit in this day or age, have no concept of the depth and height of who He is or who you are in Him. Without the indwelling of His Holy Spirit, there is no intimacy with Him. There is no impartation of His gifts, knowledge, and wisdom in your life. In other words, there is no ability to know the person of Christ without the Spirit of God being resident in you, which leaves you attempting to discover more about Him through the life of someone who is indwelt by His Spirit. But this will only afford you second hand knowledge of who He is, while God's desire is that we are filled to overflowing with His Spirit and partakers of the unexplainable riches of His glory in Christ Jesus.

"That he would grant you according to the riches of his glory, to be strengthened with might by his Spirit in the inner man; That Christ may dwell in your hearts by faith; that ye, being rooted and grounded in love, may be able to comprehend with all saints what is the breadth, and length, and depth, and height; And to know the love of Christ, which passes knowledge, that ye might be filled with all the fullness of God." (Ephesians 3:16-19)

"Herein is our love made perfect, that we may have boldness in the day of judgment: because as he is, so are we in this world." (I John 4:17)

If we would just take a moment to think about the love of God, it would not take long to realize that God has literally gone out of His way to demonstrate His love towards us. In fact, He has gone above and far beyond what we even deserve of His love. In every way imaginable, He has expressed his immeasurable love towards us in the very fact that all He has done, is doing, and shall do, is entirely for our benefit.

"For all things are for your sakes, that the abundant grace might through the thanksgiving of many redound to the glory of God." (2 Corinthians 4:15)

Because we are the focus of His love and object of His desire, there is nothing that He delights in doing more than demonstrating His love in our lives. Being the object of His love is the greatest honor and privilege that we have been afforded. Why? Because of His fervent love toward us, He did not wait until we were in Christ to demonstrate the truth of His heart to us. As a matter of fact, before we were even saved, He took the first step to release and manifest the proof of His love towards us through the death of His son Jesus.

"But God commended his love toward us, in that, while we were yet sinners, Christ died for us. Much more then, being now justified by his blood, we shall be saved from wrath through him." (Romans 5:8-9)

Yet, the death of Jesus was only the beginning of His unquenchable love towards us. There is so much more in store for us. Much more! God is not only able to give us more of Himself, but it is His earnest desire, which has been made possible, seeing that Jesus did not remain in the grave; He rose from the grave possessing all power. And with this power, He gave us power to also become the sons of God.

"But as many as received him, to them gave he gave power to become the sons of God, even to them that believe on his name" (John 1:12)

He gave us power not only to be mere children of God, but to become mature sons of God who receive the greater measure of His love and grace. There are just some things that God will only allow His sons to be partakers of rather than His little children because sons are mentally and emotionally capable of handling what children cannot handle. He desires to literally give us the Kingdom of God on earth. But children are not capable of governing His Kingdom, seeing that they lack the necessary wisdom, power, and understanding needed to govern their own lives. They are just too immature and too unfit to govern or oversee the things of God. Nevertheless, no one is ever too young or too old to receive the immeasurable love of God that He extends towards us all. Even so, God is amazing in the aspect of knowing what we are capable of handling and what we are incapable of handling. And His love will always meet us exactly where our level of development is.

"Now I say, That the heir, as long as he is a child, differs nothing from a servant, though he be lord of all; But is under tutors and governors until the time appointed of the father. Even so we, when we were children, were in bondage under the elements of the world: But when the fullness of the time was come, God sent forth his Son, made of a woman, made under the law, to redeem

them that were under the law, that we might receive the adoption of sons. And because ye are sons, God hath sent forth the Spirit of his Son into your hearts, crying, Abba, Father. Wherefore thou art no more a servant, but a son; and if a son, then an heir of God through Christ." (Galatians 4:1-8)

He knows the depths of our hearts and the limitations of our faculties as His children. But who can measure the depth of God's love towards us or test the strength of His faculties? No one can because it cannot be measured. God's love transcends space, time, and reasoning. His love cannot be measured by the standards of men nor can it be defined by theory. The manner of love that God reveals in our lives is a love that can only be experienced through an intimate relationship with Him. The depth of His love has no bounds, no limitations, or stipulations whereby it can be confined in any way. It is eternal and always actively engaged in fulfilling His will in both the natural and spiritual realms. Without His love, nothing could exist. Yet, because He loved us, we have forever become His beloved sons and partakers of His glory.

"Having predestined us unto the adoption of children by Jesus Christ to himself according to the good pleasure of his will. To the praise of the glory of his grace, wherein he hath made us accepted in the beloved." (Ephesians 1:5-6)

God's love and purpose for us is eternal as He is eternal, which means there is no end to His love for us, nor will there ever be a moment when His purpose is not operating in our lives and for the good of all mankind. He has loved us with an eternal love, so that we ourselves are also able to love with the same eternal love.

Chapter Seven
Thanks Be to God Who Gave Us Victory

The uncanny thing about our journey to destiny is that God has already secured us through His victory. In fact, He has already strategically predestined every step of our journey. We only need to walk it out by faith from the starting line to the finishing line. Are you seeing the big picture now? If not, let me help you out by declaring to you that everything God did in your life was intentional. There is nothing that transpired in your life that has taken God by surprise. Not one thing that you have done or that you have encountered has ever made God flinch in despair. Why? Because God has been and always will be in total control of your life's journey. And it is Him alone who gives you the victory with every step you take and every stride that you are willing to make.

"And we know that all things work together for good to them that love God, to them who are the called according to his purpose. For whom he did foreknow, he also did predestinate to be conformed to the image of his Son, that he might be the firstborn among many brethren. Moreover; whom he did predestinate, them he also called; and whom he called, them he also justified; and whom he justified, them he also glorified." (Romans 8:28-30)

Knowing that God has secured us in victory from the very start, our objective should continually be geared towards reaching the finish line of this journey. It must be our daily objective because the finish line is the place where everything we have endured on this journey to destiny finally comes together like a completed puzzle that has the magnitude, quality, and propensity to reveal God's glory to onlookers, spectators and others who are also participating in similar journeys. So, we are now able to see just how vital the preparation for this journey was. All the training, exercising, disciplinary dieting, and rigorous conditioning both spiritually and naturally tend to make complete sense once we reach the finish line. It was all necessary and profitable for us, as the preparation helped us to remove unnecessary weights, regulate our pace, strengthen our endurance, and complete the journey set before us. Yet, I will not sugar coat the truth and say that the preparation process was easy by any means; it was never meant to be easy. Nor will I say that the process was aimless because it was exceptionally rewarding to us, as it fulfilled God's purpose in us.

"Wherefore seeing we also are compassed about with so great a cloud of witnesses, let us lay aside every weight, and the sin which doth so easily beset us, and let us run with patience the race that is set before us, Looking unto Jesus the author and finisher of our faith; who for the joy that was set before him endured the cross, despising the shame, and is set down at the right hand of the throne of God." (Hebrews 12:1-2)

Although a rewarding process in the ultimate purpose in which it served in our lives, it was also extremely painstaking. I believe the most gruesome part of the preparation process that we had to endure on this journey to destiny was the removal of unnecessary weights in our lives. This is by far the most intense aspect of the process because it involves the dismantling and restructuring of our mind, emotions, and will. While it is beneficial to our edification in all things, it is nevertheless an extremely unpleasant process, as it produces an onslaught of psychological confrontation, emotional exhaustion, and unrelenting suppression of the will. Neither is it a one-time experience for believers. But this process is ongoing throughout the duration of our journey, since it is the method God uses to mold us into vessels that are worthy to receive His glory. He is the potter and we are the clay, so in essence we are just putty in His hands. Whatever manner of vessel He deems us to be is what we will inevitably become.

"Nay but, O man, who art thou that replies against God? Shall the thing formed say to him that formed it, why hast thou made me thus? Hath not the potter power over the clay, of the same lump to make one vessel unto honor, and another unto dishonor? (Romans 10:20-21)

Throughout this molding process, we were being internally restructured, and revamped to receive the increase flow of His Spirit, that we might prove befitting for the eternal Kingdom of God in every way possible. At times, the restructuring within us felt equivalent to a brutal conflict between opposing forces. While we ourselves wanted little to no interruption of the existing state of our internal person, God desired more for us and required more from us. He desired to make us into His eternal abode, as well as allowing us to experience His eternal glory that we might abide in Him as one.

"Neither pray I for these alone, but for them also which shall believe on me through their word; That they all may be one; as thou, Father, art in me, and I in thee, that they also may be one in us: that the world may believe that thou has sent me. And the glory which thou gave me I have given them; that they may be one, even as we are one. I in them, and thou in me, that they may be made perfect in one; and that the world may know that thou hast sent me, and hast loved them, as thou hast loved me. Father, I will that they also, whom thou hast given me, be with me where I am; that they may behold my glory, which thou hast given me: for thou loved me before the foundation of the world. O righteous Father, the world hath not known thee: but I have known thee, and these have known that thou has sent me. And I have declared unto them thy name and will declare it: that the love wherewith thou hast loved me may be in them, and I in them." (John 18:20-26)

As He restructured us internally and the steady flow of His Spirit increased within us, we were being transitioned from glory to glory. Our minds were being upgraded, so that our emotions and will could be brought into complete alignment or total agreement with His ever-increasing Spirit that had become resident in us. His will was progressively becoming our will. His thoughts were progressively becoming our thoughts. His heartbeat was progressively becoming our heartbeat. We were being made into His very own image. No longer was our life being lived for the fulfillment of self-satisfaction, but we were now living to the glory and honor of God. It was no longer our own will being done, but it was His will that was being performed in and through us. No longer were our lives governed by our own fleshly inspired thoughts, but it was the mind of Christ that now had the preeminence in overseeing the course of our lives. Nor was it our own emotions that ruled our hearts, but it was now the fruit of the Spirit that ruled and reigned in our hearts. We had become new creatures in Christ and old things were being eradicated to allow room for the new things of Christ to take root in us and flourish through us.

"But we all, with open face beholding as in a glass the glory of the Lord, are changed into the same image from glory to glory, even as by the Spirit of the Lord." (2 Corinthians 3:18)

The most intriguing part of this journey for me lies in the fact that God would give so much of Himself to us, when we were not vessels worthy enough to even stand in His presence. We had no knowledge, right or access to approach Him on any level. Yet, He was moved by His immeasurable love for us that He prepared a way to bridge the gap, which had separated us from Him since the fall of Adam. He did the unthinkable for you and me. He gave His Son Jesus Christ as a sacrifice for our sins, which afforded us the opportunity to enter the greatest and most endearing relationship ever known to mankind. It is a superlative affinity between God and man, as He made a way for us to not only be saved from the penalty of our sins but has allowed us to partake of His glory and nature, so that we might become sons and daughters to Him. We were strangers and foreigners who had no birthright in God. There was no inheritance that we were entitled to in the Kingdom of God. As sinners, we had been alienated from the things of God. Unrighteousness and death were our portion or allotment under heaven. To put it plainly, we were doomed. But God!

"For through him we both have access by one Spirit unto the Father. Now therefore ye are no more strangers and foreigners, but fellow citizens with the saints, and of the household of God." (Ephesians 2:18-19)

We have not only been given the victory through Christ, but we have been given a new citizenship in heaven. God has given us the best that He has to offer in proving His love to us. Everything that we did not deserve is exactly what we have been given in Christ. There is absolutely nothing that God has not made available to us in Christ. In fact, He has given us everything in full measure, and we only need to grow into our glorious Kingdom inheritance.

Amen.

ABOUT THE AUTHOR

Cynthia Alvarez is a dedicated servant of the Lord Jesus Christ. Her passion for the King and His Kingdom is undeniable as she continues to empower the Body of Christ in this hour. The goal of her work is to break believers out of the typical church pattern by acclimating them to the culture of the Kingdom of God. *'Revealed'* is nothing less than remarkable and life altering in every way. It is one of several books written by Cynthia Alvarez that is designed to transform lives and produce a harvest of souls that are qualified for dominion in the Kingdom of our eternal Lord and Savior Jesus Christ.

A special thanks to all who have supported the endeavors of Cynthia Alvarez with your purchase of this book. May the blessings of our Lord Jesus Christ richly increase you above measure.

Cynthia Alvarez

ABOUT THE BOOK

Revealed is nothing less than remarkable and life altering in every way. It challenges every believer's stance in God to see if they are willing to embark upon a journey that is powerful and expansive enough to transform the very foundation of their lives. Without question, the greatest decision that any believer can make in this hour is choosing to be all that he or she can be in Christ. Once this decision is made, the greatness of the Kingdom is set before them and destiny becomes attainable. The authenticity of greatness in the Kingdom of God becomes possible when believers refuse to settle for less than God offers them. As the time of Kingdom acceleration and manifestation is upon us, believers are commanded to rise in the fullness of God and take their rightful places in His Kingdom. Are you up for the challenge? Do you see yourself as being more than just a complacent believer? If so, *Revealed* is a must read, as it will catapult you forward and higher in your quest for Kingdom increase.

Cynthia Alvarez

www.ingramcontent.com/pod-product-compliance
Lightning Source LLC
Chambersburg PA
CBHW050204130526
44591CB00034B/2087